KEVIN DURANT

An Unauthorized Biography

Copyright © 2014 by Belmont & Belcourt Biographies

All rights reserved. Neither this book nor any parts within it may be sold or reproduced in any form without permission.

ISBN: 9781619840782

eISBN: 9781619841482

KEVIN DURANT

An Unauthorized Biography

TABLE OF CONTENTS

INTRODUCTION 7
THE EARLY YEARS 11
THE HIGH SCHOOL YEARS 17
COLLEGE CAREER 21
LANDING IN THE NBA 25
    2007-08 SEASON 27
    2008-09 SEASON 29
    2009-10 SEASON 33
    2010-11 SEASON 35
    2011-12 SEASON 39
    2012-13 SEASON 45
    2013-14 SEASON 53
    2014-15 SEASON 59
INTERNATIONAL CAREER 65
CHARITABLE CONTRIBUTIONS 67
ENDORSEMENTS 69
PERSONAL LIFE 73
CONCLUSION 75
STATISTICS 77
    REGULAR SEASON STATS 77
    POST SEASON STATS 77

Belmont & Belcourt Biographies

"Hard work beats talent when talent fails to work hard."

– Taras Brown

INTRODUCTION

When parents Wayne and Wanda Pratt welcomed their son, Kevin Wayne Durant, into the world on September 29, 1988 in Washington D.C., they likely envisioned great things for him. Like most parents, they probably called him special and one-of-a-kind, and hoped that he would do wonderful things both for this world and for himself.

Little did they know their son would eventually become a basketball powerhouse, dubbed as one of the best players in the world with millions of fans and more than $18 million worth of paychecks every year. He's been one of the NBA's best players since turning pro at 19 with the Seattle SuperSonics (which became the Oklahoma City Thunder after his rookie season), and he hasn't looked back since. Neither Durant nor his family could have envisioned the amount of success he would establish and all because of hard work over the years.

Kevin Durant: An Unauthorized Biography

"I never thought I would have this many people on the porch at my grandma's house. Just because I could play basketball a little bit."

– Kevin Durant

THE EARLY YEARS

In 2013, rather than gathering the media for the launch of his newest shoe design at a formal venue, Durant brought everyone over to his hometown of Seat Pleasant, Maryland to show them around the neighborhood where he had grown up and had developed his love of basketball.

Both parents were young when they started their family. Wanda was only 18 when she gave birth to Anthony (Tony), Durant's older brother, and Durant was born three years later. Just before Durant's first birthday, Wayne split, leaving his then 21-year-old wife and mother of two to raise the boys by herself. Thankfully for Wanda, her mother Barbara Davis had helped her in raising the children. Now known by the nickname "Mama Durant", Wanda eventually divorced Wayne, and went back to her maiden name, Durant, which young Kevin took as well.

In an effort to keep her sons off the streets, Wanda had her two sons spend time at the local recreation center – the Seat Pleasant Activity Center. To ensure her sons had everything they needed, Wanda worked overnight in a post office, loading mailbags onto trucks so that she could be home in time for the kids to get home from school.

Durant was so inspired by his mother's hard work, selflessness, and devotion to her family that it inspired him to work harder at basketball to ensure all of her hard work wasn't for nothing. He would do hours of drills in the afternoon, imagining himself as Vince Carter, who, at that time, played in the Toronto Raptors – Durant's favorite team.

Durant's first coach, Charles "Big Chucky" Craig, was also a huge inspiration for him when he was just 8-years-old. Craig became a father figure, going as far as taking Durant to the movies and giving him food in addition to just providing him with basketball advice and guidance.

Durant played on the PG Jaguars, the Amateur Athletic Union (AAU) team based out of Prince George's County, Maryland, and was coached by Taras "Stink" Brown. Craig was the assistant coach as well as the team's bus driver. The PG Jaguars won two national championships during the time Durant was a part of the team. When Durant was just 11, he scored 18 points in the second half of the final game. He fell in love with basketball so deeply during this time of his life that he told his mother he wanted to be in the NBA. Head Coach Brown always tried to inspire Durant, and after giving him a paper that read, "Hard work beats talent when talent fails to work hard", he made Durant write out the quote 200 times.

Brown would bring Durant to the corner of Balsamtree Drive and L Street and make him run up the hill and then walk down backwards 25 times, all while Wanda would sit in the car at the bottom and read a book. If she wanted to continue reading, she would make him do 25 more, and if he lost count, he would start all over again. It proved to be an invaluable experience for Durant, who said, "I know when I have a son and he wants to play basketball, this is the first place I'm gonna send him. I'm going to sit in my car and read a book and make him do 25 extra like I did. I'm looking forward to that day."

It was also during these early years that Durant met Michael Beasley, also a future NBA player. The two became best friends after Beasley stole the team's pizza after his very first practice (he did eventually confess the following week). Beasley's mother was a single parent, and every morning before school, she would drop him off at Durant's home for breakfast and the two would ride the bus together to school. They eventually met Chris Braswell, another future NBA player, and the three became the stars of the PG Jaguars. When Durant left for high school, Coach Brown disbanded the PG Jaguars after the 2003 season, explaining, "I didn't want to hold the kids back. They were too good."

The Seat Pleasant Activity Center was such a major part of Durant's development into the basketball player he is today that there's an entire room there dubbed "Durant's Den." Durant has donated three checks totaling $125,000 to the center and he even filmed a Nike commercial there. In addition to video game machines and televisions, "Durant's Den" is decked out in memorabilia and trophies.

THE HIGH SCHOOL YEARS

From 2002-04, Durant attended National Christian Academy in Fort Washington, Maryland, before transferring to the legendary Oak Hill Academy in Mouth of Wilson, Virginia for his junior year. He attended Oak Hill not only to work on his education, but also for its reputation as the premier high school basketball institution in the country. In fact, ESPN televised three of Durant's games with Oak Hill during that season. Durant also tried his hand at playing first base in baseball for a few games, but soon discovered baseball wasn't for him.

It was also during his time at Oak Hill when Durant learned of the tragic death of his mentor, Charles "Big Chucky" Craig at a young age of 35. Craig died on April 30,

2005 after being shot multiple times in Laurel, Maryland on Laurel-Bowie Road. Durant has worn the number 35 since college in honor of the age at which Craig had passed away. From 2005-06, Durant moved on to his senior year at Montrose Christian School in Rockville, Maryland so that he could be closer to his family.

Durant was fantastic throughout all his previous years of basketball, but it was during his senior year when he really started to shine. He averaged 23.6 points, 10 rebounds, three assists, and 2.6 blocks per game. This was compared to his junior season at Oak Hill when he averaged 19.6 points and 8.8 rebounds per game. While at Montrose, he helped lead the team to a 20-2 record which landed them the number nine spot on the *USA Today* poll of best high school teams in the country. Many recruiting services dubbed him the second best high school prospect in the United States (behind only Greg Oden).

It was after his senior year that *USA Today* and *Parade* magazine named him First Team All-American (he was named Second Team All-American the year before). Additionally, he was named Co-MVP of 2006 the McDonald's All-American Game after scoring 25 points on 10 of 17 shooting in 18 minutes.

During high school, he earned the nickname "The Durantula" and shot up to 6'9" – his current height – and his wingspan measured in at an incredible 7' 4.75" which made it easy, and continues to make it easy, for him to shoot over many fellow players. During high school, Durant wasn't about partying or hanging out with friends outside of basketball. He was so focused on basketball that he didn't have a driver's license. When he wasn't playing basketball or training, he would be at home with his mother. Durant states that he loved high school and his friends, but he jokingly told ESPN in 2009 that his one regret from that time period was never getting a triple-double (even though he had recorded a quadruple double).

COLLEGE CAREER

After a stellar high school career, Durant chose to play with the University of Texas Longhorns in Austin, Texas thanks in part to the recruitment efforts of Russell Springmann, an assistant at the University of Texas and also a Maryland native. Durant was a starter for the Longhorns during his first season in 2006-07 and helped lead his team to a record of 25 - 10. Although they made it to the Big 12 Tournament championship game where Durant was named the Tournament MVP, the Longhorns lost in overtime to the Kansas Jayhawks.

Durant played all 35 games of the season (1,255 minutes total), averaged 25.8 points per game, 11.1 rebounds per game, 1.9 blocks per game, had a 47.3 field goal percentage, 40.4 three-point field goal percentage, and an 81.6 free throw percentage. During his time out on the court, he scored 30+ points 11 times, 20+ points 30 times, and had 20 double-doubles. He scored a career-high of 37 points on four separate occasions.

After the season, Durant became the first freshman in history to not only win the Adolph Rupp Trophy, but also the John R. Wooden Award, and the Oscar Robertson Trophy. He was named as the Associated Press College Player of the Year (also the first freshman to win), Consensus National Player of the Year, the NABC Player of the Year (first freshman to win), the Naismith Men's College Player of the Year (first freshman to win), Consensus First Team All-American, and the USBWA National Freshman of the Year. Additionally, he was named the Big 12 Conference Player of the Year, was the Big 12 Freshman of the Year, made the Big 12 All-Defensive Team and the All-Big 12 First Team, was the

All-Rookie Team Pick with a unanimous vote, was the Big 12 MVP, and received First Team All-Conference honors.

Durant broke Big 12 records for many accomplishments that season, including most points scored in a season (903), 37 points in a first game for a conference game (1/6/07), 462 points in a season for conference games, most points per game for a conference game (28.9 for the season during 16 games), most field goals made in a season (157), and most field goal attempts in a game (31 on 1/16/07). He was a four time Big 12 Player of the Week and a six time Big 12 Rookie of the Week.

After making such an enormous impression on the basketball world in his freshman year, Durant had only one place to go. The NBA.

Belmont & Belcourt Biographies

"I just thought it was time to go. It's been my dream for a while. I felt I was ready."

— Kevin Durant

LANDING IN THE NBA

At 18, after his first and only year of college basketball, Durant made himself available for the 2007 NBA Draft. There was a debate about whether he or Greg Oden, the center for The Ohio State University, would be chosen first. Ultimately, however, he was chosen second by the Seattle SuperSonics in the first round as the second pick behind Oden. Portland's decision to choose Oden over Durant will likely forever be considered one of the worst draft day decisions in the history of the NBA. Rather than wearing a suit like most players at their press conferences announcing their decision to join the NBA, Durant opted to wear his practice uniform.

Belmont & Belcourt Biographies

2007-08 SEASON

In true Durant style, Kevin made moves right from the beginning of this new chapter in his life. He was selected as part of the All-Rookie First Team, was the recipient of the NBA Rookie of the Month Award on five different occasions, and was honored as the NBA's 2007-08 Rookie of the Year. In the T-Mobile Rookie Challenge game, he scored 23 points, dished four assists, and grabbed eight rebounds. On April 16, 2008 in a game against the Golden State Warriors, Durant became the youngest person, at 19 and 200 days, to score 42 points in a single game. His 42 points and 13 rebounds were both career highs. It was also his first double-double in his professional career. The SuperSonics won that game 126 – 121.

Durant was only the third teenager after LeBron James and Carmelo Anthony to average more than 20-points per game in a season. He averaged 20.3 points per game, making him the first amongst rookies and the 24th in the NBA. He also averaged 4.3 rebounds, 2.4 assists, and 1 steal. He ended up scoring 20 or more points in 44 games. He had 80 starts in all 80 games, shot at 87.3 percent from the free throw line, led his team with 75 blocks, and averaged at 2.4 assists per game.

Despite his stellar numbers, the SuperSonics had a record of 20-62 during his rookie season which landed them in 5th place of the Northwest Division and without a spot in the playoffs.

2008-09 SEASON

The 2008-09 season was one of relocation as the Seattle SuperSonics packed their basketballs and took their game to Oklahoma City, Oklahoma (renaming the team the Oklahoma City Thunder in the process). The change came after their owner, Clay Bennett, didn't get approval for a $500 million arena. After litigation involving Bennett and the city of Seattle, as well as Bennett and previous team owner, Howard Schultz, the SuperSonics were ready to move to Oklahoma City (Bennett's home town) after Oklahoma voters approved $120 million worth of tax incentives and Bennett signed a 15-year lease. According to Forbes, the team's value in 2007 was $268 million and they sold 78 percent of their tickets, but at the end of 2008, they were worth around $300 million and were selling out tickets to their new home —

Chesapeake Arena. In 2011, they were valued at $329 million, and in 2012, they were valued at $348 million.

It was during this season that Durant improved his averages, boosting up to 25.3 points per game. He also increased his rebound average to 6.5, his assists to 2.8, and his steals to 1.3. He put up 20+ points 57 times, 21 times he put up 30+ points, and three times he scored 40+ points. He also had 15 double-doubles. In the New Orleans game on February 17, he scored an incredible 47-points, a career high, but that wasn't his only personal best of the season. He also had five steals on December 13 against Dallas.

Despite his best, the team still had a losing season. For the 200-09 season, the Thunder finished with a record of

23 – 59 that put them in 5th place again in the Northwest Division and outside of the playoffs.

Belmont & Belcourt Biographies

2009-10 SEASON

In the 2009-10 season, Durant became the Oklahoma City Thunder's first All-Star. He averaged 30.1 points per game, 7.6 rebounds, 1.4 steals, and 2.8 assists. At 21 and 197 days, he was the youngest player in the history of the NBA to win a scoring title. It was the first year he averaged 30+ points and he was one of only 10 players to start in all 82 games. Durant also had 25 double-doubles, had 18 free throws without missing one (a franchise record), and 8 times he totaled 40 points or more.

Durant was also named First Team All NBA. From December 22 to February 23, he had 25 points or more in each of the 29 games, making it not only a franchise record, but the longest streak in the NBA. He was the scoring leader that year with 2,472 total points (this would not be the last time he achieved the honor). In a losing effort on December 04 versus the Celtics, he scored 36 points, putting him over the 4,000 career point mark and making him the second youngest NBA player to achieve that feat behind only LeBron James. Three different times, he was named the NBA Player of the Week.

In a remarkable turnaround, the Oklahoma City Thunder finished the 2009-10 season with a record of 50 – 32 and finished in 4th place in the Northwest Division and 8th place in the Western Conference earning them a playoff spot. They lost (2-4) in the first round to the Los Angeles Lakers (2-4).

2010-11 SEASON

Once again, Durant was named an NBA All-Star, was the NBA scoring champion, and was part of the All-NBA First Team. In December 2010 and April 2011, he was the NBA Player of the Month, and he was named the Player of the Week two separate times. Moreover, he was again the league's leading total-point scorer with 2,161 points in 78 games and averaged 27.7 points per game. He also averaged 6.8 rebounds, 2.7 assists, and 1.1 steals.

In a January 26, 2011 victory against the Minnesota Timberwolves, Durant scored a career high of 47 points and grabbed a career high 18 rebounds that game. The game on March 18, 2011 against the Charlotte Bobcats was also a high point. The Thunder beat the Bobcats 99 –

82 and it also marked his 300th NBA game. During the season, he scored 30+ points 29 times, including five times when he scored 40+ points.

During his time in the NBA to this point, Durant developed a reputation as a "nice guy". It was evident in a 2011 article by a reporter who said, "Kevin Durant the nicest young superstar the league has seen in ages. In addition to scoring tons of points and leading the Oklahoma City Thunder to the postseason, he is courteous to reporters, kind to teammates and generally seems more grounded than other players who get voted to be All-Star starters. You wouldn't mind seeing your son be his friend or your daughter bringing him home."

The Oklahoma City Thunder finished the 2010 – 2011 season with a record of 55 – 27, finished 1st in the Northwest Division and 4th overall in the Western Conference. They won the NBA Western Conference First Round (4-1) against the Denver Nuggets, and won the NBA Western Conference Semifinals (4-3) against the Memphis Grizzlies, but lost the NBA Western Conference Finals (1-4) against the Dallas Mavericks.

2011-12 SEASON

For the third year in a row, Durant was the NBA scoring champion, was named as an NBA All-Star, and was named to the All-NBA First Team. He led the NBA with 1,850 points for the season, he averaged 28 points in 66 games. In February and March, he was awarded the NBA Player of the Month.

In a February 19, 2012 win against the Denver Nuggets, Durant set a new career high of 51 points. In addition to the one 50+ point game, he had four 40+ point games, and 25 30+ point games (four of which were the first four consecutive games of the season). He had 18 double-doubles on the season, five of which took place in consecutive games from January 27 to February 04.

Durant was a three-time recipient of the NBA Western Conference Player of the Week Award this season, was a starter on the Western Conference All-Star Team, and was named the MVP of the All-Star game thanks to his 36 points and 7 rebounds.

2011 was also the year of the NBA lockout, which was the fourth one in history. In 2005, the players union and the NBA agreed on a 6-year collective bargaining agreement, which expired without resolution. The lockout started on July 01 at 12:01 am. Several players either talked about possibly going to play for overseas teams or actually signed a contract, and the International Basketball Federation (FIBA) granted permission to the players to do so considering there was no sighting of a new agreement in the near future. After several meetings and discussions over the course of months, the lockout was over on December 08, 2011 with the signing a 10-year collective bargaining agreement. The season was set to begin on December 09, 2011 at 2:00 pm EST.

Considering Durant had some extra time on his hands, he used it to his advantage. He took up all-day training sessions with his personal trainer, Justin Zormelo. The two spent so much time working on making his game even better that Zormelo would sleep on Durant's couch. When Durant was later voted league MVP, he made sure to give credit to the guy who contributed to getting him in great playing shape. He stated, "He's a big part of what I've done these last few years." Since Zormelo started Best Ball Analytics back in 2011, he's had over 30 NBA clients with whom he works individually.

In 2012, the Oklahoma City Thunder made it to the NBA Finals where they went against LeBron James and the Miami Heat. In a series that showed that Durant and superstar teammates Russell Westbrook and James Harden still had some work to do to be champions, the Thunder lost to the Heat in five games (1-4).

As he was walking off the court and through the tunnel, Durant showed just how much the loss upset him and he started to cry. In the press conference that took place after the game, he said, "It hurts. It hurts, man. We're all brothers on this team. It just hurts to go out like this. We made it to the Finals, which was cool for us, but we didn't want to just make it there... As a whole, I'm proud of the guys and how we fought all season... I wouldn't want to play for anyone else, I wouldn't want to play for any other city." While some criticized him for showing emotion after the loss, many commended him for it and stated that there was nothing wrong with his actions.

For the lockout-shortened season 2011-12 year, the Thunder went 47 – 19, which put them first in the Northwest Division and second in the Western Conference. The Oklahoma City Thunder won the first round of the NBA Western Conference (4-0) against the Dallas Mavericks, won the semifinals of the NBA Western Conference (4-1) against the Los Angeles Lakers, and won the Western Conference finals (4-2) against the mighty San Antonio Spurs.

"He's all-around, he's not just an offensive player. He does many more things for us. He's a defender, he's a rebounder, he's a passer, ball mover and a screen setter. He does all the little things that we ask Nick Collison to do. He just scores a little better than Nick."

– Scott Brooks, Thunder Head Coach

2012-13 SEASON

Once again for the fourth year in a row, Durant was named to the All-NBA first team. He averaged 28.1 points per game with 7.9 rebounds and 4.6 assists, but lost out on the total scoring title to Carmelo Anthony of the New York Knicks, who averaged 28.7 points per game and scored 1,920 total points in 67 games. However, Durant did have three triple-doubles and 18 double-doubles, scored 40+ points six times, 30+ points 33 times, and 20+ points 71 times. He was again voted onto the Western Conference All-Star Team, and in October, November and March, he was named the NBA Western Conference Player of the Month.

In a January 18, 2013 win against the Dallas Mavericks, Durant scored a career-high 52 points and connected on all 21 of his shots from the free throw line. He would end the season with an incredible 90.5 percent free throw percentage. Scott Brooks, the coach of the Thunder, spoke of him and said, "Sometimes when your shot doesn't fall, you've got to find a way to attack the basket and will yourself to get opportunities. He did that tonight and got opportunities at the free-throw line. He's an amazing player and he deserves everything that he has earned."

Durant joined the exclusive "50-40-90" club at the end of the season as he had at least a 50 percent field goal percentage, at least a 40 percent from the 3-point field goal, and a 90 percent or more free throw percentage throughout the season. He was only the sixth NBA player to reach the milestone behind Larry Bird in 1987 and 1988, Mark Price in 1989, Reggie Miller in 1994, Dirk Nowitzki in 2007, and Steve Nash in 2006, 2008, 2009, and 2010.

In a game against the Los Angeles Clippers on November, 21, 2012, Durant lived up to his nice guy image when he accidentally tossed a basketball into the stands, resulting in an elderly woman getting hit in the head as she sat courtside. Not only did he go over to see if she was okay, he kissed her on the forehead before moving on with the game. Maybe she was good luck because the Thunder ended up winning that game 117 – 111.

On January 02, 2013 in a game against the Brooklyn Nets, Durant did something that he'd never done before in his career. While that statement would usually pertain to something positive, such as achieving a career-high amount of points in a single game, this time he got ejected for the first time in his professional 400+ games. He didn't like the calls the refs were making, so in the final minutes of the game, he let referee Danny Crawford know exactly how he felt, which included an F-bomb. On his first ejection, he said, "I just told him (Crawford) I thought it was a bad call, they (officials) have quick triggers in this league now, but yes I was frustrated but I think I'm allowed to be frustrated, especially in this league with all the ups and downs."

In a January 06, 2013 game against the Raptors, which the Thunder won 104 – 92, Durant got his third technical foul in three games (the first two were at the aforementioned January 2 game). On the same day at

5:27 pm, he took to Twitter to post, "3 techs in 3 games, not like me...@kendrickperkins is a bad influence on my life lol jk..I will be better, sorry guys." His grandma was not feeling his actions on the court, and she let him know about it. He posted a text screenshot to his Instagram account of a conversation between himself and his grandma where she says, "Thunder struck again & the Sun(s) went down (great W) Love u g mom. Kev kev stop cussing so much they be showing u when u do" to which he responded, "Haha sorry grandma I be so emotional, I love u."

Yet another woman sitting courtside got hit by a flying ball at the February 10, 2013 game against the Suns (the Thunder won 97 – 69). After getting smacked in the head, the woman had her head down with her hair over her face, and Durant went over and patted her head to make sure she was alright.

Throughout the season, Durant kept continuing to rack up the technical fouls. On March 05, 2013 in a game against the Los Angeles Lakers where the Thunder won 122 – 105, he earned his 13th technical foul. Three more and he earns himself a suspension. His 13th happened when he made a comment to official Joey Crawford. He later said, "Joey is a good ref and I respect him a lot. But hopefully that gets rescinded. All I asked him was, verbatim, is 'Can I talk to you?' and he got me with one."

On April 12, 2013, Durant was smacked with a big fine after he did a "menacing gesture" while playing against the Golden State Warriors. He did a throat slash and prayer motions with his hand, resulting in a $25,000 fine. He had 31 points that game, as well as 10 rebounds and 8 assists, and the Thunder won 116 – 97. In the postgame, he explained, "Kill 'em and pray for 'em after the game," then followed up by saying, "It's nothing against the team I'm playing against. Come out with a mindset and be friends after the game."

In April, rapper Jay-Z founded sports agency Roc Nation Sports, and in June, he became the first NBA player to sign with them, a move that would prove to be quite profitable for him in the future.

The Oklahoma City Thunder finished the 2012-13 season with a record of 60 – 22 that put them 1st in the Northwest Division and 1st on the Western Conference.

They went on to win the NBA Western Conference First Round playoff series (4-2) against the Houston Rockets, but lost the NBA Western Conference Semifinals (1-4) against the Memphis Grizzlies.

2013-14 SEASON

In the 2013-14 season, Durant started in all 81 games and had 3 triple-doubles and 27 double-doubles. He also averaged 32 points, 5.5 assists (a career-high), 1.3 steals, and 7.4 rebounds.

For the fifth time, he was named to the NBA Western Conference All-Star Team and named to the All-NBA First Team, and he was also named the Kia NBA MVP. In November, December, January and March, he was the Western Conference Player of the Month. He was the recipient of the 2014 Best NBA Player ESPY Award, as well as the 2014 Best Male Athlete ESPY Award.

It was another big year for points from the superstar, who had the highest scoring month of his entire career (an average of 35.9 points per game) in January when he also had 12 consecutive games of 30+ points. From January 07 through to April 08, he scored 25+ points in each of the 41 games. He scored 30+ points 47 times this season with 14 40+ point games and even two 50+ point games. On January 17, 2014 in a game against the Golden State Warriors, he scored a career-high 54 points. The Thunder won that game 127 – 121.

Durant was also the league leader for minutes played (3,122), field goals (849), field goal attempts (1,688), free throws (703), free throw attempts (805), points (2,593), player efficiency rating (29.8), usage pct (33), offensive win shares (14.8), value over replacement player (8.0), offensive box plus/minus (8.0), win shares per 48 minutes (.295), and win shares (19.2).

Although he had many positive accomplishments, he picked up his 14th technical foul followed by his 15th technical foul one night later. He ended up having his 15th technical foul rescinded, which put him just two technical fouls away from a one game suspension. Fast forward to April 11, 2014 to the Thunder's game against the New Orleans Pelicans when Durant got yet another technical foul which, once again, put him just one technical foul away from a game suspension.

The Oklahoma City Thunder finished the 2013-14 season with a record of 59 – 23 that put them 1st in the Northwest Division and 2nd in the Western Conference to the San Antonio Spurs. They won the NBA Western Conference First Round (4-3) against the Memphis Grizzlies and won the NBA Western Conference Semifinals (4-2) against the Los Angeles Clippers, but lost the NBA Western Conference Finals (2-4) against the San Antonio Spurs.

Kevin Durant: An Unauthorized Biography

Belmont & Belcourt Biographies

"How can I lose when I came here with nothing?"

– Kevin Durant

2014-15 SEASON

Rather than racking up the points and accomplishments in the 2014-15 season, Durant spent the majority of his time doing one thing: recovering.

On October 12, 2014, the Oklahoma City Thunder announced that Kevin Durant had a Jones fracture in his right foot, which is a broken bone at the base of his small toe. Their general manager, Sam Presti, said, "From what I've been told, a Jones fracture is the most common surgical procedure performed on NBA players as of late. It has happened enough so that there is enough of a body of work to look at an average recovery time." At the time, they were saying it was likely he would miss six to eight weeks. Presti also explained, "We're really fortunate to be catching it when we're catching it. Very fortunate that Kevin notified us yesterday, and we're catching it kind of on the front end, before this became a little bit more of an acute issue."

Durant underwent surgery, and on October 16, 2014, he took to Twitter and posted, "Successful surgery, thanks for all the prayers and concerns! Headed back to okc. Move em." Of his injury, he said in October, "It's definitely a different experience for me. I've never been injured before, but the Thunder's been great to get me to the best surgeon, and rehab has been going well so far. Everything is progressing, and I'm looking forward to these next few weeks of getting better."

Throughout the season, he had soreness in his foot as was to be expected, but then just eight games after his return, he sprained his right ankle in a December 18, 2014 game against the Warriors which the Thunder lost 114 – 109. He ended up missing six games. He explained,

"I was a little nervous. But I knew when I got up and started walking it felt good. So I just wanted to make sure with the X-rays everything was good." Between the ankle sprain and the broken bone in his foot, he missed 23 games.

When he returned to the court on December 31, 2014, Durant ended up scoring 44 points, and had 7 assists and 10 rebounds to help the Thunder barely pull off the 137 – 134 win over the Suns in overtime. That game was the highest scoring one in the season. According to ESPN Stats & Info, his big points earned him yet another accomplishment. On January 01, 2015 at 12:12 am, they tweeted, "Kevin Durant's 44 points are the most in NBA history by a player who didn't appear in his team's previous 5+ games."

Come January 25, 2015, Durant had yet another injury. In a game against the Cavaliers, he sprained the big toe on his left foot and had to miss four games. Once again, he made it back on the court, but was out again after informing his team on February 19, 2015 that he was having soreness in his right foot where he had the surgery to replace the broken bone. He had another procedure to ease the discomfort that stemmed from one of the screws rubbing against the cuboid bone. Due to his injuries, he played in only 27 games in the 2014-15 season.

On February 14, 2015, when talking to the media at All-Star Weekend in New York, he was asked about the job security of his coach, Scott Brooks, and he had some pretty choice words and didn't hesitate to let everyone know just how he feels. He fired off, "You guys really don't know s---," then later on when he was asked what type of questions he wanted the media to focus on, he said, "To be honest, man, I'm only here talking to y'all because I have to. So I really don't care. Y'all not my friends. You're going to write what you want to write. You're going to love us one day and hate us the next. That's a part of it. So I just learn how to deal with y'all."

It's clear that he's gotten more comfortable with expressing his feelings and being more vocal whether it's to refs or reporters. It was just the day before on February 13 when he said, "I am just learning to be myself, not worrying about what everybody else says. I am going to make mistakes. I just want to show kids out here that athletes, entertainers, whoever, so-called celebrities, we aren't robots. We go through emotions and go through feelings and I am just trying to express mine and try to help people along the way. I am not going to sit here and tell you that I am just this guy that is programmed to say the right stuff all the time and politically correct answers. I am done with that."

INTERNATIONAL CAREER

Durant was chosen to play on the 2012 U.S. Olympic basketball team where the U.S. team came back with a gold medal. As usual, he made history by scoring 156 total points; the most points ever scored in a single Olympics by a player for the United States. He averaged 19.5 points and 5.8 rebounds in all 8 games (all of which he started).

His father, Wayne, was watching his son play in the Olympics from his home in Annapolis, while his mother, Wanda, was in the stands in London cheering like a proud mom.

Belmont & Belcourt Biographies

CHARITABLE CONTRIBUTIONS

In 2013, Durant was so affected by the devastation that happened as a result of tornadoes that moved through Oklahoma that he donated $1 million to the American Red Cross. Their regional CEO, Janienne Bella, said, "The Red Cross relies on its donors to perform its mission in relieving human suffering following disasters. Mr. Durant's gift and support to Oklahoma comes at a time of great need and we're forever thankful for his generosity." The Thunder also donated $1 million as did the NBA and the National Basketball Players Association.

In 2014, Durant founded the Kevin Durant Charity Foundation, which partnered with the KIND snack company. During the summer, the foundation served over 3,000 children in foster care and those who are homeless.

ENDORSEMENTS

As of the end of 2014, Durant had the title of having the most endorsement deals of any NBA player. In November 2014, he became Sonic's first athlete ambassador where he had to come up with his own dishes as part of his endorsement deal. Of the partnership, Sonic's chief marketing manager, Todd Smith, said, "We feel really good about this partnership because Kevin is uniquely aligned with what we do and who we are as a brand," and the President and chief of branding and strategy for Roc Nation, Michael Yormark, explained, "Everything that Kevin pitches comes from an authentic point of view. When it comes to grab-and-go food, KD's a Sonic guy."

In August 2014, there was a rivalry between Under Armour and Nike over who would get the Durant endorsement, and Nike won out. Their original seven year, $60 million deal was ready to expire, but after a new offer was put on the table, he decided to stick with them. In February 2015, the footwear giant and Durant teamed up to create a sneaker that pays homage to the basketball player's late Aunt Pearl who died in 2001 from lung cancer. The sneakers are white, which is the color of lung cancer awareness, features an angel wing strap over the laces, and is detailed with pink and gold accents, including having gold swooshes across the front. The shoes hit the market on February 19, 2015. It's not the first time he's designed sneakers in her honor. They're actually the fourth in a series, one for every year since 2012.

Earlier in 2004, he teamed up with Orange Leaf Frozen Yogurt making it his first equity based endorsement deal. In 2014, he also landed an endorsement deal with Sparkling Ice, a carbonated water drink that has zero calories. Regarding his deal, he explained to ESPN, "I've always challenged myself on the basketball court, but this offseason is really the first year I'm challenging myself off of it -- on the business side. This is a brand I drink every day that I love and I wanted to be a part of it. I want to help them get to the next level."

Durant previously had an endorsement deal with Gatorade, but in 2013, news broke that the contract would not be renewed. He does, however, still have his endorsement with KIND bars. Go further back to 2011 and he had signed an endorsement deal with Panini

Authentic, a company that offers signature memorabilia, and in 2010, he teamed up with Skullcandy. Other endorsement deals he currently holds are with Sprint, 2K Sports, and BBVA Compass.

PERSONAL LIFE

In July 2013, news broke that Durant was engaged to Monica Wright, a guard for the WNBA's Minnesota Lynx. The pair met back in 2006, and they've both been extremely quiet over the years about whether their relationship was romantic or platonic – that is until Wright confirmed their engagement. However, the pair reportedly split in early 2014 as confirmed by Wright herself. Of the split, she said, "I was engaged last year and it kind of changed that relationship big time because I was going in a direction that unfortunately a lot of people aren't willing to sacrifice their lifestyle for." Many were speculating that it was over religious beliefs, however, in an interview with *GQ* magazine in early 2015, Durant opened up and explained, "I had a fiancée, but...I really didn't know how to, like, love her, you know what

I'm saying? We just went our separate ways." He touched on how the engagement happened and said, "We was just hanging out, chilling. And I felt the energy. I felt, *I need to do this right now.* And I just did it. I was like...*We're engaged right now? We're about to get married?* So I was just like, cool! I love this girl. But I didn't love her the right way."

The 26-year-old went on to talk about his thoughts that many others – celebrities and non-celebrities alike – have at one point or another. He said, "I go to sleep at night, like, 'Am I gonna be alone forever?'" and followed up by saying, "Am I gonna be alone forever? Am I gonna have kids?" and "I feel like there's no hope. But I still gotta have faith."

CONCLUSION

Back in 2009 during an interview with ESPN, a then 20-year-old Durant was asked what advice he would give young athletes, and he gave a very inspirational answer, especially for someone so young. He said, "Easiest thing, and it sounds cliché: Always work hard, believe in yourself and remember that you can't go through this on your own. You have to have teammates, coaches and parents you believe in and who believe in you. Because it's hard. As you get older, players get better and you start to even out. That's what the separates the good level from the great level."

Despite the injuries, he has continued to battle forward. He's a basketball player who seems genuinely humbled by his success, and has clearly proven to have a deep love and respect not only for the game, but for those who have helped him along the way. With that positive attitude, who knows how far he'll continue to go.

Through basketball, Kevin Durant knows that he has a platform to help others and make an impact in the community.

STATISTICS

REGULAR SEASON STATS

Season	TEAM	GP	PTS	FG%	3P%	FT%	OREB	DREB	REB	AST	STL	BLK
2007-08	SEA	80	20.3	43	28.8	87.3	0.9	3.5	4.4	2.4	1	0.9
2008-09	OKC	74	25.3	47.6	42.2	86.3	1	5.5	6.5	2.8	1.3	0.7
2009-10	OKC	82	30.1	47.6	36.5	90	1.3	6.3	7.6	2.8	1.4	1
2010-11	OKC	78	27.7	46.2	35	88	0.7	6.1	6.8	2.7	1.1	1
2011-12	OKC	66	28	49.6	38.7	86	0.6	7.4	8	3.5	1.3	1.2
2012-13	OKC	81	28.1	51	41.6	90.5	0.6	7.3	7.9	4.6	1.4	1.3
2013-14	OKC	81	32	50.3	39.1	87.3	0.7	6.7	7.4	5.5	1.3	0.7
2014-15	OKC	27	25.4	51	40.3	85.4	0.6	6.0	6.6	4.1	0.9	0.9
Overall		569	27.3	48.1	37.9	88.1	0.8	6.1	6.9	3.5	1.2	1

POST SEASON STATS

Season	TEAM	GP	PTS	FG%	3P%	FT%	OREB	DREB	REB	AST	STL	BLK
2009-10	OKC	6	25	35	28.6	87.1	1.3	6.3	7.7	2.3	0.5	1.3
2010-11	OKC	17	28.6	44.9	33.9	83.8	1.1	7.1	8.2	2.8	0.9	1.1
2011-12	OKC	20	28.5	51.7	37.3	86.4	0.7	6.8	7.4	3.7	1.5	1.2
2012-13	OKC	11	30.8	45.5	31.4	83	0.6	8.4	9	6.3	1.3	1.1
2013-14	OKC	19	29.6	46	34.4	81	1.3	7.6	8.9	3.9	1	1.3
Overall		73	28.9	46.2	34.1	83.9	1	7.3	8.2	3.8	1.1	1.2

Made in the USA
San Bernardino, CA
21 April 2017